Adding Whole Numbers

Table of Contents

Adventure! Go for the Gold!		ii
Lesson 1	Properties of Addition	1
Hands-On Lesson 2A	Adding to Make a 10 Using Counters	5
Lesson 2	Adding Three 1-Digit Numbers	9
Lesson 3	Adding 2-Digit Numbers with No Regrouping	13
Hands-On Lesson 4A	Modeling Addition with Regrouping Using Base-10 Pieces	17
Lesson 4	Adding 2-Digit Numbers with Regrouping	19
Lesson 5	Adding Three 2-Digit Numbers with No Regrouping	23
Lesson 6	Adding Three 2-Digit Numbers with Regrouping	27
Lesson 7	Adding 3-Digit Numbers with No Regrouping	31
Lesson 8	Adding 3-Digit Numbers with Regrouping	35
Lesson 9	Adding Multi-Digit Numbers with Regrouping	39
Lesson 10	Estimating Sums	43
Gizmos™ Lesson 11A	Target Sum Card Game (Multi-digit Addition)	47
Lesson 11	Reasonableness and Estimation	49
End of Module Review		53
Extra Practice		55
Glossary		61
Student Progress Chart		63

Cover art: ©Purestock, Purestock, Getty Images

ISBN 978-1-4168-6119-5

Copyright © 2009 by Voyager Expanded Learning, Inc.

All rights reserved. No part of this publication may be reproduced or transmitted in any form or by any means, electronic or mechanical, including photocopy, recording, or any information storage and retrieval system, without permission in writing from the publisher.

Printed in the United States of America   09 10 11 12 13 14 PAD   9 8 7 6 5 4 3 2 1

ADVENTURE!

Go for the Gold!

The first modern Olympic Games were in 1896. Only 241 athletes were there. The 2008 Olympics were in China. More than 11,000 people were in them. Since 1896, the United States has won more than 900 gold medals.

Medal Count

In this adventure, you will learn about Olympic gold medals. Answer each problem.

1. Look at the next page. The table shows the number of gold medals won by the United States in the Summer Olympic Games. How many gold medals has the United States won since 2000?

2. The Summer Olympic Games were in the United States 4 times. They were in Los Angeles 2 times, St. Louis 1 time, and Atlanta 1 time. How many total gold medals did the United States win in these places?

3. The Summer Olympic Games were in 3 other cities twice—Paris, Athens, and London. How many medals did the United States win in Paris? In Athens? Where did the United States win more medals, Paris or Athens?

4. In 2004, the United States had the top rank. U.S. athletes received 35 gold medals, 39 silver medals, and 29 bronze medals. What was the total medal count?

5. In 2004, swimmer Michael Phelps won 6 gold medals and 2 bronze medals. In 2008, he won 8 gold medals. How many medals has Michael won in all?

Further Adventure

6. The gold medal for the 2008 Summer Olympics is a round disc. It has designs on the front and back. It measures between 2 and 3 inches across. The medal weighs about 5 ounces. Design your own Olympic gold medal. Then write a short paragraph with at least 3 sentences to tell about your design.

Level D Module 2 • Adding Whole Numbers

U.S. Summer Olympics Gold Medals

Year	Location	Gold Medals
1896	Athens	11
1900	Paris	20
1904	St. Louis	80
1908	London	23
1912	Stockholm	23
1920	Antwerp	41
1924	Paris	45
1928	Amsterdam	22
1932	Los Angeles	41
1936	Berlin	24
1948	London	38
1952	Helsinki	40
1956	Melbourne	32
1960	Rome	34
1964	Tokyo	36
1968	Mexico City	45
1972	Munich	33
1976	Montreal	34
1980	Moscow	0
1984	Los Angeles	83
1988	Seoul	36
1992	Barcelona	37
1996	Atlanta	44
2000	Sydney	40
2004	Athens	35
2008	Beijing	36

New Vocabulary
Commutative Property of Addition
Associative Property of Addition

Lesson 1

Properties of Addition

Name _____ Class _____ Date _____

GET STARTED

① 5 + 2 = _____

② 8 + 6 = _____

③ a. 🌼🌼🌼🌼🌼 + 🌼🌼

_____ + _____ = _____ flowers

b. 🌼🌼 + 🌼🌼🌼🌼🌼

_____ + _____ = _____ flowers

④ a. (🐟🐟🐟 + 🐟🐟) + 🐟 = 🐟🐟🐟🐟🐟 + 🐟

(_____ + _____) + _____ = _____ + _____ = _____ fish

b. 🐟🐟🐟 + (🐟🐟 + 🐟) = 🐟🐟🐟🐟🐟 + 🐟🐟🐟

_____ + (_____ + _____) = _____ + _____ = _____ fish

BUILD THE CONCEPT

★★★ + ★    +

3 + 1 = _____   _____ + _____ = _____

Level D Module 2 • Adding Whole Numbers   1

Lesson 1

TRY IT TOGETHER

Find each sum. Use the Commutative Property of Addition to write another addition fact.

5   6 + 3 = _____   _____ + _____ = _____

6   3 + 8 = _____   _____ + _____ = _____

Find each sum. Use the Associative Property of Addition to write another addition fact.

7   4 + (1 + 5) = 4 + _____ = _____

(_____ + _____) + _____ = _____ + _____ = _____

8   (2 + 7) + 3 = _____ + 3 = _____

_____ + (_____ + _____) = _____ + _____ = _____

WORK ON YOUR OWN

Add Whole Numbers Using the Commutative and Associative Properties of Addition

Using Symbols	Using Words
6 + 1 = 1 + 6 6 + 1 = 7 1 + 6 = 7	**Commutative Property of Addition:** Changing the order of the addends does not affect the sum.
(4 + 3) + 1 = 4 + (3 + 1) (4 + 3) + 1 = 7 + 1 = 8 4 + (3 + 1) = 4 + 4 = 8	**Associative Property of Addition:** Grouping the addends in any order does not affect the sum.

SKILL BUILDING: NEW AND REVIEW

Find each sum. Use the Commutative Property of Addition to write another addition fact.

9   7 + 4

10   5 + 8

Find each sum. Use the Associative Property of Addition to write another addition fact.

11   (5 + 2) + 3

12   1 + (6 + 2)

Find each sum.

13   8 + 9

14   7 + 7

PROBLEM-SOLVING: NEW AND REVIEW

Solve each problem.

15   At the school store, Bobby bought a pencil for 5¢ and an eraser for 2¢. Justin bought a whistle for 2¢ and a sticker for 5¢. How much did each boy spend?

16   Selma's brother has 5 teddy bears. Selma has 2 teddy bears and 1 stuffed rabbit. The addition problem (5 + 2) + 1 shows how many total stuffed animals they have. Use the Associative Property of Addition to write and solve another addition problem.

17   In a soccer game, the home team scored 3 points in the first half and 2 points in the second half. The away team scored 2 points in the first half and 3 points in the second half. Who won the game? Explain.

18   Nancy has 8 blue marbles and 6 purple marbles. How many marbles does she have in all?

Lesson 1

CHECK UP

Answer each question.

1. Use the Commutative Property of Addition to find the missing number.

$6 + ? = 9$ and $? + 6 = 9$

a. 4
b. 7
c. 3
d. 2

2. $2 + (5 + 5) = ?$

a. 9
b. 12
c. 2
d. 10

3. Which answer choice in problem 2 is the least reasonable? Explain. _____
_____
_____

EXPLAIN IT

Justin found the sum using the following steps. He says that he used both properties of addition. Is he correct? Explain.

$8 + (5 + 2) = 8 + (2 + 5) = (8 + 2) + 5 = 10 + 5 = 15$

_____
_____
_____

4. Using the numbers 4, 1, and 2 and the Associative Property of Addition, write two addition problems that add the three numbers. Then solve each to show that they have the same sum. _____
_____
_____

Lesson 1 • Properties of Addition

Lesson 2A

Adding to Make a 10 Using Counters

Name _____ Class _____ Date _____

① 8 + 2 = _____

② 8 + 3 = _____

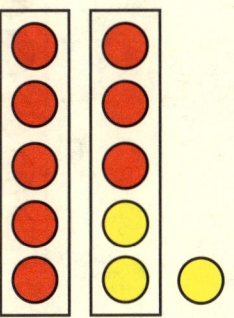

DISCOVER

③ 7 ●●●●●●●
3 ●●●
+2 ●●

7 counters + _____ counters = _____ counters

_____ counters + 2 counters = _____ counters

Level D Module 2 • Adding Whole Numbers

Lesson 2A

4.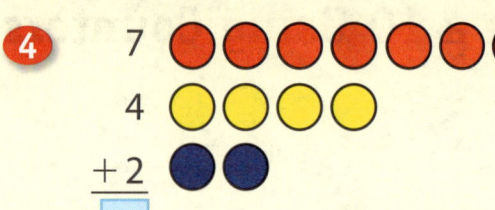

7 counters + _____ counters = 10 counters

1 counter + _____ counters = _____ counters

10 counters + _____ counters = _____ counters

5.

How many counters will you put into the tens frame for the first addend? _____

How many counters will you put into the tens frame for the second addend? _____

How many counters from the second addend will not fit in the tens frame? _____

What addition problem can you write for the counters that would not fit in the tens frame and for the third addend?
_____ + _____ = _____

What addition problem can you write for the counters in the tens frame and the sum of the other counters? _____ + _____ = _____

Lesson 2A

DISCOVER BOX

Use a tens frame and 3 different colors of counters to show 7 + 4 + 5. Then show how to model 4 + 5 + 7. Explain how the models of the 2 problems are alike.

_____
_____
_____
_____

EXPLORE MORE

Use counters and a tens frame to find each sum.

6)   6   **7)**   6   **8)**   9
     4   5   4
  +1   +3   +5
   ☐   ☐   ☐

Level D Module 2 • Adding Whole Numbers

New Vocabulary
make a 10

Lesson 2

Adding Three 1-Digit Numbers

Name _____ Class _____ Date _____

GET STARTED

1 a. $8 + (4 + 1) = (8 + 4) + 1$ b. $10 + 5 = 5 + 10$

_____   _____
_____   _____

2 $6 + 4 + 3 = (\_\_\_ + \_\_\_) + \_\_\_$

    6 ⟩
    4 ⟩
 + 3 → + ___
 ___

3 $8 + 3 + 3 = (\_\_\_ + \_\_\_) + \_\_\_ = \_\_\_ + (\_\_\_ + \_\_\_)$

    8 →
    3 ⟩
 + 3 ⟩ + ___
 ___

4 $4 + 8 + 6 = (\_\_\_ + \_\_\_) + 6 =$
$(\_\_\_ + \_\_\_) + 6 = \_\_\_ + (\_\_\_ + 6)$

    8 →
    4 ⟩
 + 6 ⟩ + ___
 ___

BUILD THE CONCEPT

$(4 + 3) + 6$ $(3 + 4) + 6$ $3 + (4 + 6)$

  4 ⟩   3 ⟩   3 →
  3 ⟩   4 ⟩   4 ⟩
+ 6 → + ___   + 6 → + ___   + 6 ⟩ + ___
___   ___   ___

Level D Module 2 • Adding Whole Numbers   9

Lesson 2

TRY IT TOGETHER

Find each sum.

5   3 + 5 + 9

       3
       5
   + 9 → + ___
   _____

6   5 + 3 + 5 =
(____ + ____) + ____ =
(____ + ____) + ____ =
____ + (____ + ____)

     3
     5
  + 5 → + ___
  _____

7   5 + 2 + 8

   →
+ ___ → + ___

8   7 + 2 + 9

   →
+ ___ → + ___

WORK ON YOUR OWN

Add Three 1-Digit Whole Numbers   HOW TO

Using Symbols	Using Words
1. (**7** + **8**) + 2 = **15** + 2 OR 7 + (**8** + **2**) = 7 + **10**	Add the first two addends, or add the two addends that make a 10.
2. (**7** + **8**) + 2 = 15 + **2** = 17 OR 7 + (8 + 2) = **7** + 10 = 17	Add that sum to the remaining addend.

10   Lesson 2 • Adding Three 1-Digit Numbers

Lesson 2

SKILL BUILDING: NEW AND REVIEW

Find each sum.

9   5 + 2 + 5

10   6 + 2 + 1

11   3 + 3 + 4

12   6 + 4 + 7

13   2 + 9 + 1

14   5 + 7 + 4

15   9 + 6

16   7 + 4

17
```
   4
   5
 + 3
 ___
```

18
```
   8
   2
 + 7
 ___
```

PROBLEM-SOLVING

Using a Number Line

Nora ran 6 miles on Saturday. She ran 4 miles on Sunday. She ran 5 miles on Monday. How many miles did she run in all?

a. **Find:** how many miles Nora ran in all

b. **How?** Use a number line.

c. **Solve.** Start at 0. Count 6 units. Then count 4 more units. Finally, count 5 more units.

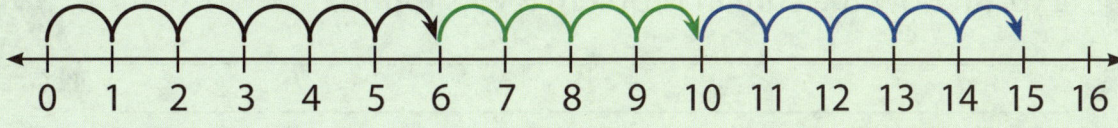

6 + 4 + 5 = _____

Nora ran _____ miles.

d. Is the answer reasonable? Explain. _____
_____
_____

Lesson 2

Module Adding Whole Numbers
Activity Add Three 1-Digit Numbers

PROBLEM-SOLVING: NEW AND REVIEW

Solve each problem.

19 In three games, Yawna's scores are 6, 4, and 2 points. What is her total score?

20 Amy has 3 pencils. Perry has 5 pencils. Mark has 8 pencils. How many pencils do they have?

21 Cameron read 8 books last month. Lisa read 7 books. Wayne read 2 books. How many books did they read?

22 Allison bought 2 lollipops at the store on Wednesday and 6 lollipops on Thursday. Paul bought 6 lollipops on Wednesday and 2 lollipops on Thursday. Who has more lollipops? Explain.

CHECK UP

Answer each question.

1 What are the missing numbers?
6 + 7 + 2 = ___ + 2 = ___

   a. 13; 33   **b.** 8; 10

   c. 13; 15   **d.** 9; 11

2 Find the sum.
7 + 4 + 3 = ?

   a. 14   **b.** 112

   c. 10   **d.** 13

3 Explain how the sum in problem 2 was found.
_____
_____
_____
_____

4 Complete the statement: 6 + _____ + 4 = 13 + 4 = 17.

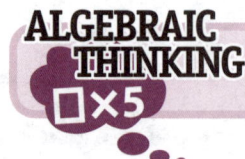

Lesson 3

Adding 2-Digit Numbers with No Regrouping

Name _____ Class _____ Date _____

GET STARTED

① 32 _____ tens _____ ones

② 59 _____

③ 5 + 2 = _____

④ 6 + 3 = _____

⑤ 65 + 32

```
   65
 + 32
 ____
```

⑥ 74 + 15

```
   74
 + 15
 ____
```

⑦ 28 + 41

```
 + ____
 ____
```

BUILD THE CONCEPT

The coins show how to add 32 and 24.

 +  =

Dimes	Pennies		Dimes	Pennies		Dimes	Pennies
Tens	Ones	+	Tens	Ones	=	Tens	Ones

32 + 24 = _____

Lesson 3

TRY IT TOGETHER

Find each sum.

8. 63
    + 24

9. 28
    + 50

10. 70 + 14

    +____

WORK ON YOUR OWN

HOW TO

Add 2-Digit Numbers with No Regrouping

Using Symbols	Using Words
1. 62 + 27 　62 + 27	Write the numbers one under the other with the place values lined up.
2. 　6**2** + 2**7** 　　**9**	Add the digits in the ones column. Write the sum in the ones column under the equal bar.
3. 　**6**2 + **2**7 　**8**9	Add the digits in the tens column. Write the sum in the tens column under the equal bar.

14 Lesson 3 • Adding 2-Digit Numbers with No Regrouping

Lesson 3

Go to VmathLive.com
Module Adding Whole Numbers
Activity Add Two 2-Digit Numbers

SKILL BUILDING: NEW AND REVIEW

Find each sum.

⑪ 62
  + 14
  ———

⑫ 32
  + 65
  ———

⑬ 10
  + 76
  ———

⑭ 47
  + 52
  ———

⑮ 25
  + 34
  ———

⑯ 73
  + 21
  ———

⑰ 34 + 32

⑱ 82 + 16

⑲ 57 + 31

⑳ 8 + 6

㉑ 6 + 2

㉒ 7 + 5

PROBLEM-SOLVING: NEW AND REVIEW

Solve each problem.

㉓ Amanda planted tulips in her garden. She planted 21 yellow tulips and 27 purple tulips. How many total tulips did Amanda plant?

㉔ Damian bought an eraser for 30 cents. Natalie bought a pen for 45 cents. How much did they spend in all?

㉕ There are 26 students in one class and 21 students in the other class. How many students are in both classes?

㉖ Three friends played basketball at recess. Cammie scored 4 points, Jason scored 2 points, and Eric scored 8 points. How many total points did they score?

Level D Module 2 • Adding Whole Numbers

Lesson 3

CHECK UP

Answer each question.

1 What is the sum of 35 and 24?

  a. 58   b. 59
  c. 52   d. 11

2 The Tigers scored 13 points in the first half of the game and 14 points in the second half. How many points did the Tigers score?

  a. 37 points   b. 47 points
  c. 27 points   d. 1 point

3 Which answer choice in problem 1 is the least reasonable? Explain. _____
_____
_____

Explain how to find the sum of 46 and 53.
_____
_____
_____
_____

4 Find the next three numbers in the pattern. Explain.

21, 32, 43, 54, _____, _____, _____

_____
_____

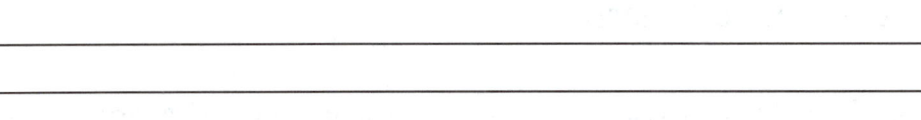

Lesson 4A

Modeling Addition with Regrouping Using Base-10 Pieces

Name _____ Class _____ Date _____

①   21
   + 32

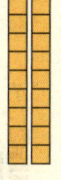

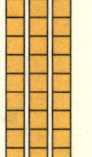

②   52
   + 27

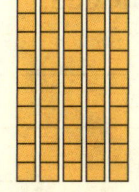

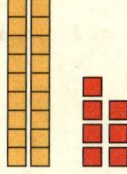

Level D Module 2 • Adding Whole Numbers   17

Lesson 4A

DISCOVER

3) 27
  + 35

4) 48
  + 17

DISCOVER BOX

Explain how to find the sum of 58 and 23 using base-10 pieces.

_____
_____
_____
_____

EXPLORE MORE

Use base-10 pieces to model each addition problem. Then find each sum.

5) 37
  + 24

6) 66
  + 18

7) 19
  + 36

Hands-On Lesson 4A • Modeling Addition with Regrouping Using Base-10 Pieces

New Vocabulary
regroup

Lesson 4

Adding 2-Digit Numbers with Regrouping

Name _____ Class _____ Date _____

GET STARTED

1. 576   a. _____   b. _____   c. _____

2. 8
    5
   + 4
   ___

3. 46 + 43

     46
   + 43
   ___

4. 27 + 45

    1
    27
   + 45
   ___

5. 56 + 17

   + ___

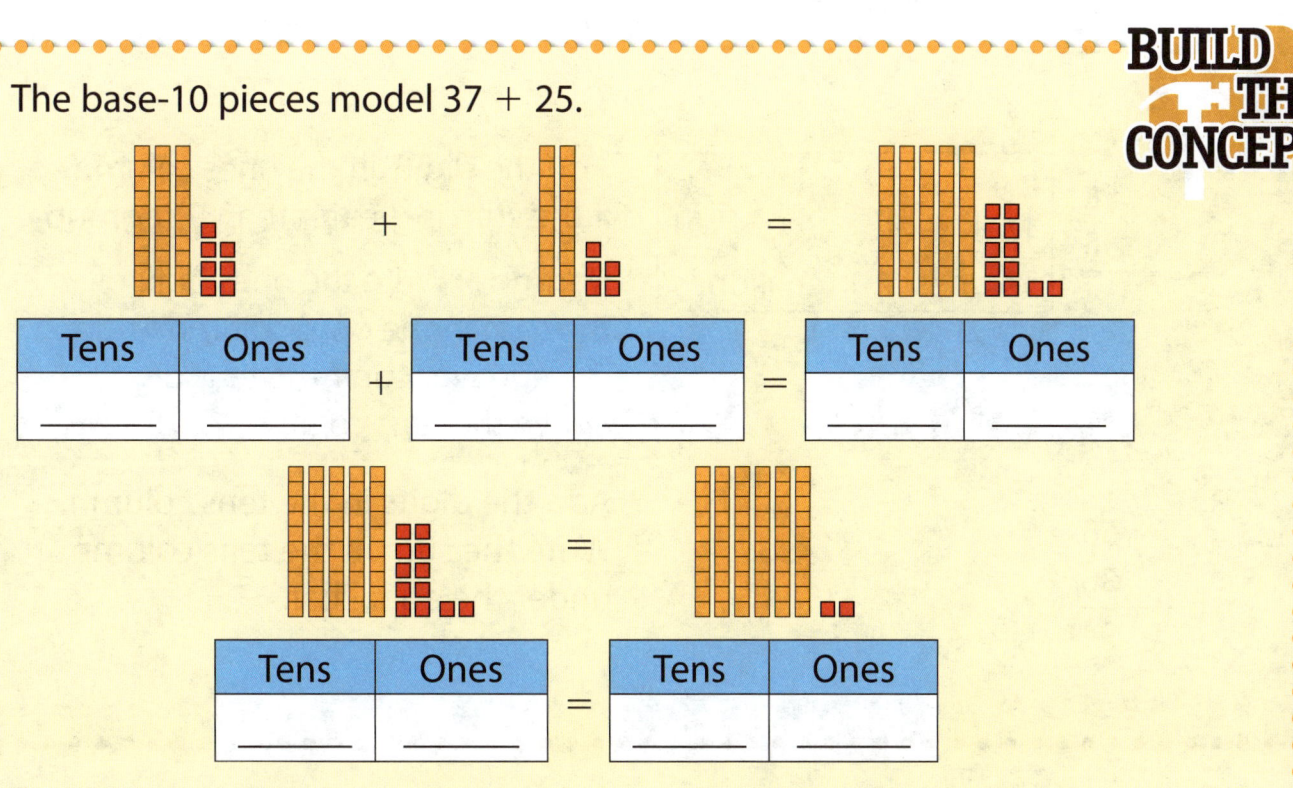

The base-10 pieces model 37 + 25.

Tens	Ones		Tens	Ones		Tens	Ones
		+			=		

Tens	Ones		Tens	Ones
		=		

37 + 25 = _____

BUILD THE CONCEPT

Level D Module 2 • Adding Whole Numbers   19

Lesson 4

TRY IT TOGETHER

Find each sum. Regroup as needed.

6   28
    + 59

7   32
    + 49

8 45 + 29

    + ___

WORK ON YOUR OWN

Add 2-Digit Numbers with Regrouping

HOW TO

Using Symbols	Using Words
1. 58 + 36 58 + 36	Write the numbers one under the other with the place values lined up.

2.   ¹
  58 | 8 + 6 = 14
+ 36 | 14 > 9
    4 | 14 ones = 1 ten 4 ones
	Add the digits in the ones column. If the sum is greater than 9, regroup.
	
	Regroup: Write the ones digit of the sum in the ones column under the equal bar and the tens digit above the tens column.

3.   ¹
  58
+ 36
  94
	Add the digits in the tens column. Write the sum in the tens column under the equal bar.

Lesson 4

SKILL BUILDING: NEW AND REVIEW

Find each sum. Regroup as needed.

9. 65
  + 28

10. 29
  + 13

11. 57
  + 26

12. 36
  + 45

13. 74
  + 16

14. 45
  + 29

15. 52 + 17

16. 43 + 16

17. 34 + 23

Choosing an Operation

Ted sold 26 chocolate cupcakes and 19 vanilla cupcakes. How many total cupcakes did Ted sell?

a. **Find:** how many total cupcakes Ted sold

b. **How?** Choose an operation.

c. **Solve.** This problem is about finding a total. Choose addition to solve.

  ☐
  26 ← number of chocolate cupcakes sold
 + 19 ← number of vanilla cupcakes sold
  ☐ ← total number of cupcakes sold

Ted sold _____ cupcakes.

d. **Is the answer reasonable? Explain.** _____
_____
_____

Level D Module 2 • Adding Whole Numbers

Lesson 4

Go to VmathLive.com

Module Adding Whole Numbers
Activity Add Two 2-Digit Numbers: Regroup

PROBLEM-SOLVING: NEW AND REVIEW

Solve each problem.

18 Connor sold 36 apple pies and 25 banana pies. How many fruit pies did he sell in all?

19 Shawna wrote the following number sentence: Explain Shawna's mistake. What is the correct answer?

```
  18
+ 22
-----
 310
```

20 Kelsey made 12 birthday invitations yesterday. Today she made 11 more invitations. If Kelsey mails all of her invitations, how many will she send?

21 Jennifer has 27 stickers. Paige has 56. If they put their stickers together, how many stickers will they have?

CHECK UP

Answer each question.

1 What is the sum of 54 and 27?

    a. 50   **b.** 71

    c. 81   **d.** 91

2 Jeff read 15 pages of his book before recess. He read 18 more pages before he went home. How many pages did Jeff read during the day?

    a. 23 pages   **b.** 213 pages

    c. 53 pages   **d.** 33 pages

3 For problem 1, which is the correct way to write the addends vertically? Explain.

```
  54          27
+ 27   or   + 54
```

4 Explain why it is important when adding multi-digit numbers to write the numbers one under the other.

Lesson 5

Adding Three 2-Digit Numbers with No Regrouping

Name _____ Class _____ Date _____

GET STARTED

1) 425   a. _____   b. _____   c. _____

2) 5 + 4 + 1 = _____

3) 63 + 25

4) 25 + 33 + 21

$$\begin{array}{r} 25 \\ 33 \\ +\ 21 \\ \hline \end{array}$$

5) 20 + 44 + 32

+ ____

BUILD THE CONCEPT

Use the number lines to find the sum of 12, 51, and 33.

Add the tens: 10 + 50 + 30 = _____

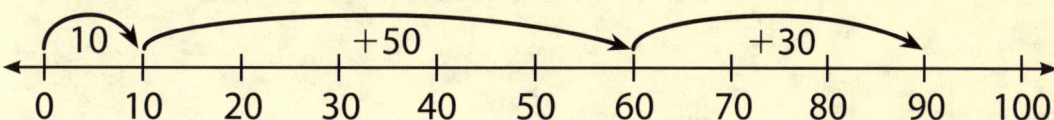

Add the ones to the sum of the tens: 90 + 2 + 1 + 3 = _____

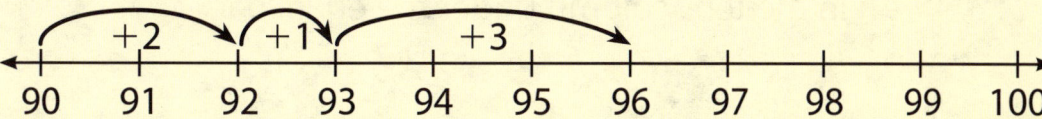

12 + 51 + 33 = _____

Level D Module 2 • Adding Whole Numbers

Lesson 5

TRY IT TOGETHER

Find each sum.

6   13
       31
   + 55

7   24
       42
   + 20

8   23 + 41 + 25

            +

WORK ON YOUR OWN

HOW TO

Add Three 2-Digit Numbers with No Regrouping

Using Symbols	Using Words

1.   42 + 15 + 21
 	
      42
      15
 + 21
	Write the numbers one under the other with the place values lined up.

2.   42
        15
    + 21
         8
	Add the digits in the ones column. Write the sum in the ones column under the equal bar.

3.   42
        15
    + 21
       78
	Add the digits in the tens column. Write the sum in the tens column under the equal bar.

Go to VmathLive.com Module Adding Whole Numbers Activity Add Three 2-Digit Numbers

Lesson 5

SKILL BUILDING: NEW AND REVIEW

Find each sum.

9
```
  62
  23
+ 14
----
```

10
```
  31
  15
+ 41
----
```

11
```
  10
  12
+ 21
----
```

12
```
  22
  15
+ 21
----
```

13
```
  23
  12
+ 40
----
```

14
```
  10
  16
+ 20
----
```

Find each sum. Regroup as needed.

15 39 + 56

16 64 + 28

17 47 + 19

PROBLEM-SOLVING: NEW AND REVIEW

Solve each problem.

18 The table shows how many newspapers Peter delivers each day. How many newspapers does Peter deliver Saturday, Sunday, and Monday?

Day	Newspaper
Saturday	22
Sunday	35
Monday	21

19 Kari buys 2 sticks of chewing gum, 5 candy bars, and 3 lollipops from the concession stand. How many total items did Kari purchase from the concession stand?

20 Tony has 30 star stickers, 14 heart stickers, and 23 sun stickers. How many stickers does Tony have in all?

21 Nathan walks 23 laps around the track. Angelina walks 13 laps, and Carlos walks 12 laps. How many total laps did they walk around the track?

Level D Module 2 • Adding Whole Numbers

Lesson 5

Answer each question.

1 What is 22 + 14 + 11?

    a. 42   b. 47

    c. 45   d. 46

2 Maria practices playing the piano for 25 minutes on Monday, 30 minutes on Tuesday, and 40 minutes on Wednesday. In all 3 days, how many minutes did Maria practice?

    a. 85 minutes   b. 65 minutes

    c. 95 minutes   d. 15 minutes

3 Which answer choice in problem 2 is the least reasonable? Explain. _____
_____

Explain how to find the sum of 11, 34, and 20.
_____
_____
_____

4 Maggie writes the number 21 in the box. What is the sum?

55 + 13 + ☐

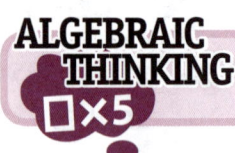

Lesson 5 • Adding Three 2-Digit Numbers with No Regrouping

Lesson 6

Adding Three 2-Digit Numbers with Regrouping

Name _____ Class _____ Date _____

GET STARTED

1 793   a. _____   b. _____   c. _____

2
```
   9
   6
+  4
-----
```

3 56 + 37
```
   56
+  37
-----
```

4 46 + 32 + 17
```
    1
   46
   32
+  17
-----
```

5 34 + 27 + 32
```

+  
-----
```

BUILD THE CONCEPT

The base-10 pieces show how to add 27, 38, and 13.

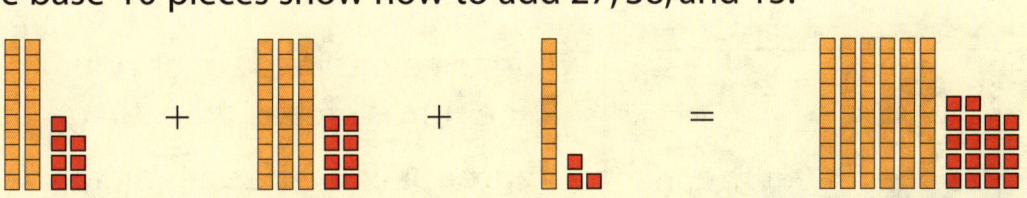

27   +   38   +   13   =

Tens	Ones
____	____

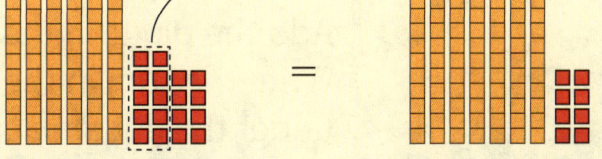

Tens	Ones		Tens	Ones
____	____	=	____	____

27 + 38 + 13 = _____

Level D Module 2 • Adding Whole Numbers   27

Lesson 6

TRY IT TOGETHER

Find each sum. Regroup as needed.

6)
```
   17
   46
+  25
─────
```

7)
```
   38
   46
+  19
─────
```

8) $29 + 54 + 12$

```
+ ___
─────
```

WORK ON YOUR OWN

Add Three 2-Digit Numbers with Regrouping   **HOW TO**

Using Symbols	Using Words

1. $48 + 19 + 26$
 	
  48
  19
 + 26
	Write the numbers one under the other lining up the place values.

2.
 ²
  4**8**
  1**9** $8 + 9 + 6 = 23$
 + 2**6** $23 > 9$
 ─────   23 ones = 2 ten 3 ones
     3
	Add the digits in the ones column. If the sum is greater than 9, regroup.
	
	 Regroup: Write the ones digit of the sum in the ones column under the equal bar and the tens digit above the tens column.

3.
 ²
  48
  19
 + **2**6
 ─────
  93
	Add the digits in the tens column. Write the sum in the tens column under the equal bar.

Lesson 6

SKILL BUILDING: NEW AND REVIEW

Find each sum. Regroup as needed.

9. 25
    45
    + 18
    ―――

10. 37
    25
    + 20
    ―――

11. 18
    37
    + 26
    ―――

12. 52
    36
    + 24
    ―――

13. 43
    17
    + 11
    ―――

14. 15
    21
    + 56
    ―――

15. 74 + 13 + 12

16. 8 + 6 + 7

17. 57 + 28

PROBLEM-SOLVING

Using a 4-Step Plan

Katie had $17 left over after the fair. She spent $15 on her ticket and $18 on rides. How much money did Katie bring to the fair?

a. **Find:** how much money Katie brought to the fair

b. **How?** Add how much money Katie had left over and how much she spent on her ticket and rides.

c. **Solve.**

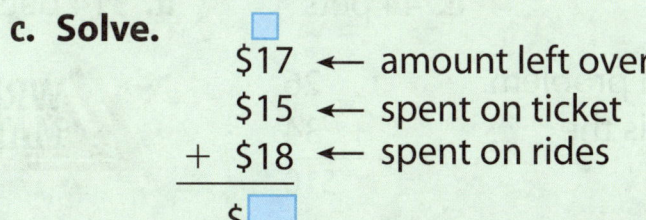

```
    ☐
  $17  ← amount left over
  $15  ← spent on ticket
+ $18  ← spent on rides
―――――
  $☐
```

Katie brought $_____ to the fair.

d. **Is the answer reasonable? Explain.** _____
_____
_____

Level D Module 2 • Adding Whole Numbers   29

Lesson 6

Go to VmathLive.com

Module Adding Whole Numbers
Activity Add Three 2-Digit Numbers: Regroup

PROBLEM-SOLVING: NEW AND REVIEW

Solve each problem.

18 Al spent $10 on his ticket, $23 on rides and food, and had $18 left over. How much did Al bring to School Fun Day?

19 Marietta has 11 DVDs, Jamie has 16 DVDs, and Shannon has 13 DVDs. How many total DVDs do the 3 have?

20 Ty walked 6 miles on Monday and 8 miles on Tuesday. Eva walked 8 miles on Monday and 6 miles on Tuesday. Who walked farther?

21 Joe counted 89 books about dinosaurs at the school library. Sue counted 46 books about airplanes, 36 books about trucks, and 18 books about trains. Who counted more books? Explain.

CHECK UP

Answer each question.

1 What is the sum of 22, 17, and 38?

   a. 67   b. 617

   c. 76   d. 77

2 A survey shows that a third-grade class has 18 dogs, 12 cats, and 14 hamsters. In all, how many pets does the third-grade class have?

   a. 40 pets   b. 64 pets

   c. 44 pets   d. 314 pets

3 Jamie completed this addition problem. Explain Jamie's mistake. What is the correct answer?

$$\begin{array}{r} 26 \\ +\ 34 \\ \hline 510 \end{array}$$

_____

_____

4 Tyler said he will have to regroup ones for tens in the addition problem 59 + 34 + 62. How does he know this?

_____

_____

Lesson 7

Adding 3-Digit Numbers with No Regrouping

Name _____ Class _____ Date _____

1 967   a. _____   b. _____   c. _____

2 23 + 64

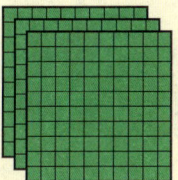

3 264 + 123

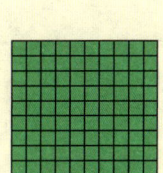

4 526 + 372

BUILD THE CONCEPT

Use base-10 pieces to add 312 and 123.

Hundreds	Tens	Ones
___	___	___

+

Hundreds	Tens	Ones
___	___	___

=

Hundreds	Tens	Ones
___	___	___

312 + 123 = _____

Level D Module 2 • Adding Whole Numbers

Lesson 7

TRY IT TOGETHER

Find each sum.

5. 354
     + 424
     ─────

6. 236
     + 602
     ─────

7. 227 + 731

     +_____
     ──────

WORK ON YOUR OWN

HOW TO

Add 3-Digit Numbers with No Regrouping

Using Symbols	Using Words
1. 473 + 125 473 + 125 ─────	Write the numbers one under the other lining up the place values.
2. 47**3** + 12**5** ───── **8**	Add the digits in the ones column. Write the sum in the ones column under the equal bar.
3. 4**7**3 + 1**2**5 ───── **9**8	Add the digits in the tens column. Write the sum in the tens column under the equal bar.
4. **4**73 + **1**25 ───── **5**98	Add the digits in the hundreds column. Write the sum in the hundreds column under the equal bar.

Lesson 7

SKILL BUILDING: NEW AND REVIEW

Find each sum.

⑧ 462
  + 314

⑨ 535
  + 254

⑩ 107
  + 781

⑪ 474 + 512

⑫ 256 + 342

⑬ 733 + 214

⑭ 37 + 21

⑮ 63 + 55

⑯ 42 + 27

PROBLEM-SOLVING: NEW AND REVIEW

Solve each problem.

⑰ Visitors to the Botanical Gardens bought 426 flowering plants and 362 vegetable plants. How many total plants did the visitors buy?

⑱ Three people ran for town mayor. The results are shown in the table. How many people voted for Ms. Adams or Mr. Brown?

Candidates	Votes
Ms. Adams	231
Mr. Brown	237
Mr. Johnson	329

⑲ Kim has 123 Canadian stamps and 225 English stamps in her stamp collection. How many total stamps does she have?

⑳ Nina collects sports cards. She has 143 baseball cards and 154 football cards. How many sports cards does Nina have?

Lesson 7

CHECK UP

Answer each question.

1 What is the sum of 325 and 424?

a. 769   b. 749
c. 99   d. 3,674

2 This year, 435 books were sold at the book fair. Last year, 260 books were sold. How many books were sold this year and last year?

a. 695 books   b. 795 books
c. 690 books   d. 175 books

3 Which answer choice in problem 2 is the least reasonable? Explain. _____
_____
_____

Explain how to find the sum of 235 and 612. What is the sum?
_____
_____
_____
_____

4 What is the value of the missing addend?

```
  246
+ ___
  398
```

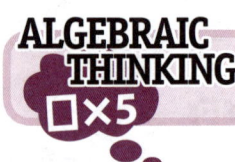

Lesson 7 • Adding 3-Digit Numbers with No Regrouping

Lesson 8

Adding 3-Digit Numbers with Regrouping

Name _____ Class _____ Date _____

GET STARTED

① 563   a. _____   b. _____   c. _____

② 36 + 57

```
   36
+  57
------
```

③ 486 + 249

```
   486
+  249
------
```

④ 677 + 193

```
+ ___
```

BUILD THE CONCEPT

Regroup ones for tens. Then regroup tens for hundreds.

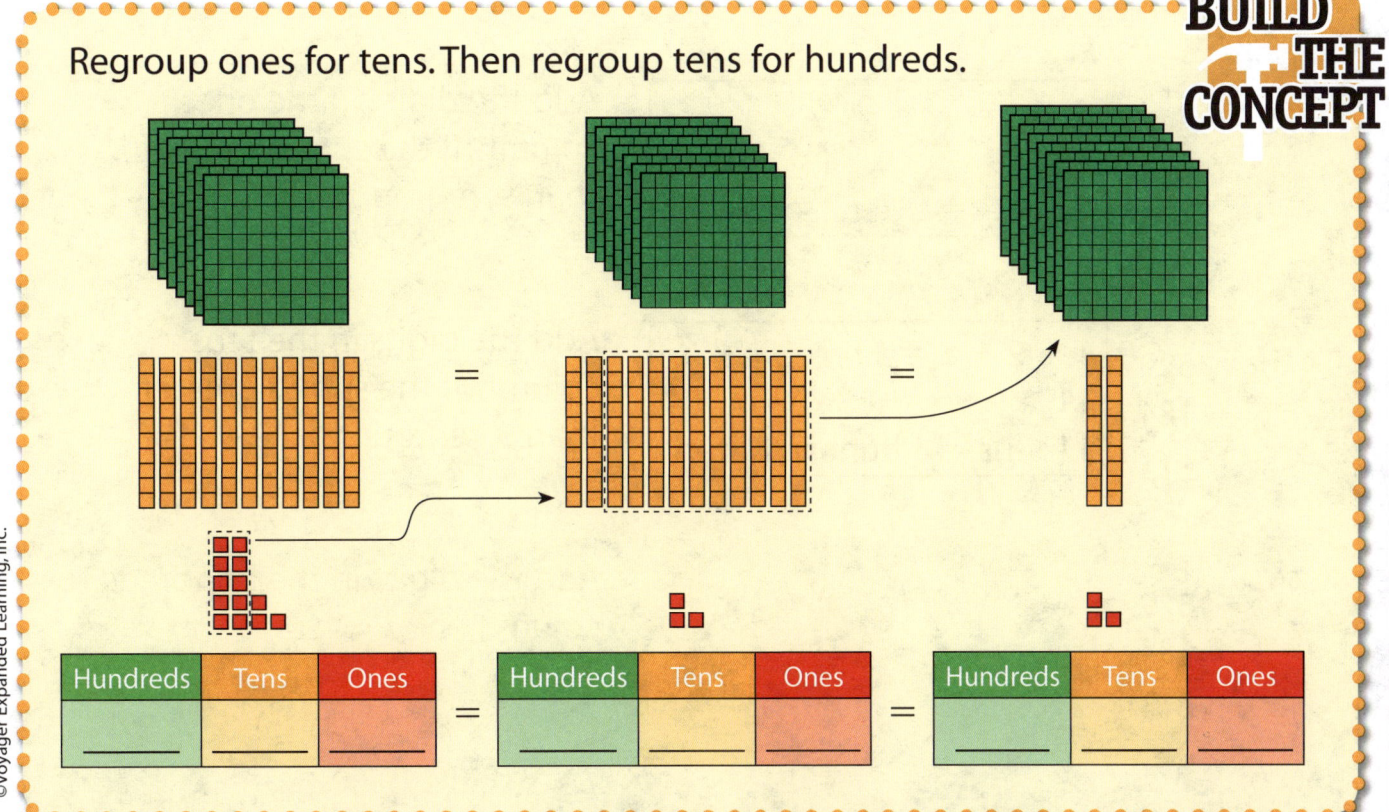

Level D Module 2 • Adding Whole Numbers   35

Lesson 8

TRY IT TOGETHER

Find each sum. Regroup as needed.

5. 265
     + 458

6. 592
     + 239

7. 273 + 461

     +_____

WORK ON YOUR OWN

Add 3-Digit Numbers with Regrouping

HOW TO

Using Symbols	Using Words
1. 629 + 184 　629 + 184	Write the numbers one under the other lining up the place values.
2. ¹ 　62**9** + 18**4** 　　**3**　　9 + 4 = 13 　　　　　13 > 9 　　　　　13 ones = 1 ten 3 ones	Add the digits in the ones column. If the sum is greater than 9, regroup.
3. ¹¹ 　6**2**9 + 1**8**4 　**1**3　　1 + 2 + 8 = 11 　　　　11 > 9 　　　　11 tens = 1 hundred 1 ten	Add the digits in the tens column. If the sum is greater than 9, regroup.
4. ¹¹ 　**6**29 + **1**84 　**8**13	Add the digits in the hundreds column.

Lesson 8 • Adding 3-Digit Numbers with Regrouping

Lesson 9

Adding Multi-Digit Numbers with Regrouping

Name _____ Class _____ Date _____

GET STARTED

1)   45
    32
 + 25
 _____

2)   742
    107
 + 113
 _____

3) 114 + 32 + 47

    114
     32
 + 47
 _____

4) 423 + 125 + 70

 +_____

BUILD THE CONCEPT

A place value chart can be used to add multi-digit numbers. This place value chart is used to add 72, 593, and 265.

Hundreds	Tens	Ones
5	9	3
2	6	5
+	7	2
Sum		

72 + 593 + 265 = _____

Level D Module 2 • Adding Whole Numbers   39

Lesson 9

TRY IT TOGETHER

Find each sum. Regroup as needed.

5) 92 + 317
+ ___

6) 741 + 89
+ ___

7) 924 + 36 + 608
+ ___

WORK ON YOUR OWN

HOW TO

Add Multi-Digit Numbers with Regrouping

Using Symbols	Using Words

1. 419 + 378 + 65
 	
   419
   378
+ 65
	Write the numbers one under the other lining up the place values.

2.   ²
   41**9**
   37**8**
+ 6**5**
     2
 	
9 + 8 + 5 = 22
22 ones = 2 tens 2 ones
	Add the digits in the ones column. If the sum is greater than 9, regroup.

3. ¹²
   4**1**9
   3**7**8
+ **6**5
   62
 	
2 + 1 + 7 + 6 = 16
16 tens = 1 hundred 6 tens
	Add the digits in the tens column. If the sum is greater than 9, regroup.

4. ¹²
   419
   378
+ 65
  862
	Add the digits in the hundreds column.

Lesson 9 • Adding Multi-Digit Numbers with Regrouping

Go to VmathLive.com Module: Adding Whole Numbers Activity: Add Multi-Digit Numbers 1 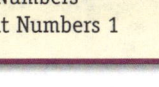 Lesson 9

SKILL BUILDING: NEW AND REVIEW

Find each sum. Regroup as needed.

8 118 + 56

9 298 + 423 + 55

10 907 + 35 + 84

11 340 + 38 + 73

12 692 + 24

13 843 + 458 + 17

14 78 + 432

15 624 + 236 + 310

16 96 + 87 + 92

PROBLEM-SOLVING: NEW AND REVIEW

Solve each problem.

17 The store sold 204 books the first day, 89 the second day, and 157 the third day. How many books did the store sell during the 3 days?

18 Ty's family traveled 422 miles the first day and 398 miles the second day. How many miles did Ty's family travel those 2 days?

19 Keiko is throwing her softball. The first time she throws the ball 108 feet, the second time 89 feet, and the third time 110 feet. How many feet did she throw the ball all 3 times?

20 There are 48 birds, 273 insects, and 165 reptiles at the Nature Center. How many animals are at the Nature Center in all?

Level D Module 2 • Adding Whole Numbers

Lesson 9

CHECK UP

Answer each question.

1. What is the sum of 76, 54, and 507?

    a. 691   b. 527

    c. 637   d. 1,807

2. Sean dribbled the basketball 312 times Friday, 529 times Saturday, and 93 times on Sunday. How many times did Sean dribble the ball on Friday, Saturday, and Sunday?

    a. 944 times   b. 934 times

    c. 1,411 times   d. 824 times

3. Which answer choice in problem 1 is the least reasonable? Explain. _____

_____

EXPLAIN IT

To add 371, 158, and 46, Nina wrote the following:

$$\begin{array}{r} \overset{1}{}371 \\ 158 \\ +\ 46 \\ \hline 989 \end{array}$$

Explain Nina's mistake. What is the correct sum?

_____

_____

_____

---

4. Write the missing ones digit in the second addend.

$$\begin{array}{r} \overset{1}{}2\ 4 \\ +\ 6\ \square \\ \hline 9\ 3 \end{array}$$

Lesson 10

Estimating Sums

Name _____ Class _____ Date _____

GET STARTED

1. 315
    268
    + 124
    _____

2. 315 ⟶ _____
    268 ⟶ _____
    124 ⟶ _____

3. 315 ⟶ 300
    268 ⟶ 300
    + 124 ⟶ + 100
    _____

BUILD THE CONCEPT

Estimate the sum: 238 + 574.

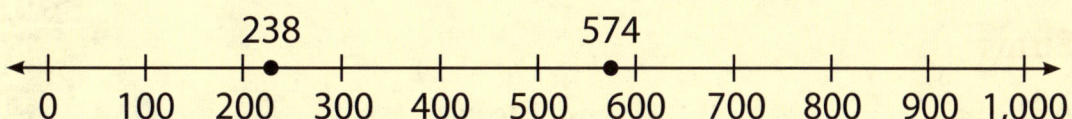

238 is between 200 and 300.
238 is closer to _____.
238 rounded to the nearest hundred is _____.

574 is between 500 and 600.
574 is closer to _____.
574 rounded to the nearest hundred is _____.

Add the rounded addends.
238 + 574
 ↓   ↓
_____ + _____ = _____

238 + 574 is about _____.

Level D Module 2 • Adding Whole Numbers 43

Lesson 10

TRY IT TOGETHER

Estimate each sum.

4)
```
  284 →
   18 →
+  47 →   + _____
-----
```

5)
```
  245 →
  618 →
+ 127 →   + _____
-----
```

6) 227 + 341 + 456
```
  227 →
  341 →
+ 456 →   + _____
-----
```

WORK ON YOUR OWN

Estimate Sums

HOW TO

Using Symbols	Using Words
1. Estimate the sum of 583, 42, and 250. 583 → **600** 250 → **300** + 42 → + **40**	Round each number to its greatest place value.

2. 600
   300
+ 40
―――
   940
 	
583 + 42 + 250 is about 940.
	Add the rounded numbers.

44 Lesson 10 • Estimating Sums

Lesson 10

SKILL BUILDING: NEW AND REVIEW

Estimate each sum.

7   225
     + 468

8   115
     + 487

9   36
     + 72

10   31
         62
     +   24

11   291
         112
     +   245

12   367
         185
     +   39

Find each sum. Regroup as needed.

13 619 + 223

14 534 + 91

15 242 + 453

PROBLEM-SOLVING

Choosing an Operation

Mr. Daniels drove 341 miles on Friday, 259 miles on Saturday, and 95 miles on Sunday. About how many total miles did Mr. Daniels drive on those 3 days?

   a. **Find:** about how many miles Mr. Daniels drove

   b. **How?** Choose an operation.

   c. **Solve.** This problem is about finding a total,   341 →
      or sum. Choose addition to estimate the sum.   259 →
                                                           + 95 → + _____

   Mr. Daniels drove about _____ miles.

   d. **Is the answer reasonable? Explain.** _____
   _____
   _____

Level D Module 2 • Adding Whole Numbers

Lesson 10

Go to VmathLive.com

Module: Adding Whole Numbers
Activity: Estimate Sums

PROBLEM-SOLVING: NEW AND REVIEW

Solve each problem.

16 There are 117 players in the baseball league, 284 players in the football league, and 93 players in the basketball league. About how many total players are in the 3 leagues?

17 The softball team sold 285 candy bars and 367 jars of jam for its fund-raiser. About how many total items were sold?

18 What is the actual number of items that were sold in problem 17?

19 Beth, Jillian, and Leanne are sisters. Beth is 18 years old. Jillian is 15 years old. Leanne is 12 years old. What is the estimated sum of their ages?

CHECK UP

Answer each question.

1 Two numbers have a sum of about 500. What are 2 possible numbers?

    a. 320; 235   **b.** 145; 489

    c. 467; 521   **d.** 58; 276

2 A new bike costs $265. A new helmet costs $97. About how much would it cost to buy the bike and helmet?

    a. about $362   **b.** about $300

    c. about $400   **d.** about $500

3 In problem 2, why is the exact answer not the correct answer choice? _____

4 Which problem's estimated sum will be greater than the exact sum? Explain.

    a. 164 + 79   **b.** 235 + 41

46   Lesson 10 • Estimating Sums

Lesson 11A

Target Sum Card Game (Multi-digit Addition)

Name _____ Class _____ Date _____

> **Gizmos Log In Instructions**
> When you are told, log in to the Gizmos as follows:
> • Log in to VmathLive™ using your Username and Password.
> • Select the Gizmos tab.
> • Click on the Target Sum Card Game (Multi-digit Addition) Gizmo link.

GET READY

Round each number to the nearest ten.

1. 38 _____
2. 64 _____
3. 45 _____

DISCOVER

4. Click Change game. Pull down the Game menu and select Custom settings. In the box next to Random, type 150. Under Digit Cards, click on the circle for Pick cards yourself.

   Then click Let's play!

   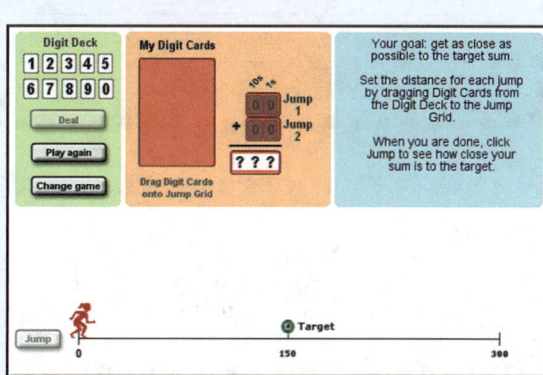

   a. From the Digit Deck, click and drag the cards for 8, 5, 4, and 2 onto the mat under My Digit Cards.

   Goal: Make two 2-digit numbers that have a sum close to 150.

   What digits would you put in the tens place? _____ and _____

   b. Use the remaining digit cards to complete the 2-digit numbers in the ones place. Record the numbers. _____

   Drag the digit cards onto the Jump Grid to make the numbers.

   c. Click Jump. Is your distance the closest possible? _____

©Voyager Expanded Learning, Inc.

Level D Module 2 • Adding Whole Numbers   47

Lesson 11A

5. Click Change game. Under Digit Cards, click on the circle for Random draw. Then click Let's play! Click Deal. If there are any 0 cards, click Play again and start over.

Drag to create two 2-digit numbers whose sum is closest to 150.

Click Jump. Is your distance the closest possible? _____

If not, rearrange the cards and try again.

DISCOVER BOX

Suppose you were dealt the cards 5, 7, 5, and 8. Your target for the jump is 180. Use rounding to explain why it is not possible to reach the target exactly.

_____
_____
_____

EXPLORE MORE

Use the Gizmo to play again.

6. Click Change game.

In the box next to Random, type 200.

Under How many jumps? click on the circle for 3.

Click Let's play! Click Deal.

Your goal is to find a sum as close as possible to 200. Drag the cards to make three 2-digit numbers. _____

Record the numbers. _____ Add to predict the sum. _____

Click Jump. Is your distance the closest possible? _____

If not, rearrange the cards and try again.

Lesson 11

Reasonableness and Estimation

Name _____ Class _____ Date _____

1) 110 →
    187 →
    + 16 → + ____

2) 345 →
    505 →
    + 169 → + ____

3) Maria practiced playing the piano for 25 minutes on Monday, 30 minutes on Tuesday, and 40 minutes on Wednesday. In all 3 days, how many minutes did Maria practice playing the piano?

   a. 85 minutes   b. 65 minutes
   c. 95 minutes   d. 15 minutes

4) This year, 435 books were sold at the book fair. Last year, 260 books were sold. How many books were sold this year and last year?

   a. 695 books   b. 795 books
   c. 895 books   d. 175 books

Lesson 11

TRY IT TOGETHER

Eliminate unreasonable answers. Solve each problem.

5 A new bike costs $265. A new helmet costs $97. How much does it cost to buy the bike and helmet?

    a. $362   **b.** $300

    c. $400   **d.** $590

6 Ana's class recycled 247 items. Omar's class recycled 198 items. How many items did both classes recycle?

    a. 247 items   **b.** 445 items

    c. 335 items   **d.** 49 items

WORK ON YOUR OWN

Use Estimation to Check for Reasonableness in Multiple-Choice Questions

Students used 418 blue balloons and 274 green balloons to decorate their school. How many balloons did the students use in all?

    ~~a. 144 balloons~~   **b.** 692 balloons

    c. 682 balloons   ~~d. 6,812 balloons~~

1. **Find:** the number of balloons the students used in all

2. **How?** Estimate the sum. Eliminate unreasonable answers. Then find the exact sum.

3. **Solve.**

    $$\begin{array}{r}418\\+\,274\\\hline\end{array} \longrightarrow \begin{array}{r}400\\+\,300\\\hline 700\end{array}$$

    144 balloons and 6,812 balloons are unreasonable answers. They are not within 100 of 700.

    418 + 274 = 692; answer choice b. 692 balloons

4. **Is the answer reasonable? Explain.** Yes, the answer is reasonable; 692 is within 100 of 700.

SKILL BUILDING: NEW AND REVIEW

Eliminate unreasonable answers. Solve each problem.

7. The Tigers scored 13 points in the first half of the game and 14 points in the second half. How many total points did the Tigers score?

   a. 37 points   b. 47 points   c. 27 points   d. 11 points

8. Jeff read 15 pages of his book before recess. He read 18 more pages before he went home. How many pages did Jeff read during the day?

   a. 63 pages   b. 213 pages   c. 53 pages   d. 33 pages

9. The third-grade students have 18 dogs, 12 cats, and 14 hamsters. In all, how many pets do the third-graders have?

   a. 84 pets   b. 64 pets   c. 44 pets   d. 314 pets

Estimate each sum.

10. $29 + 163 + 508$

11. $659 + 234$

12. $87 + 45$

PROBLEM-SOLVING: NEW AND REVIEW

Solve each problem.

13. Kevin purchased a stereo for $237 and speakers for $298. About how much total money did Kevin spend?

14. May earned $16 for mopping, $11 for dusting, and $22 for ironing. She thinks she made about $85. Is May's estimate reasonable? Explain.

15. There are 197 boys and 223 girls on a field trip. About how many boys and girls are on a field trip?

16. Amy counted 287 license plates. Jack counted 417 plates. Greg counted 84 plates. About how many plates did they count altogether?

Lesson 11

CHECK UP

Answer each question.

1. Tatiana's family went on a vacation. The first airplane they took flew 238 miles. The second airplane flew 395 miles. How many total miles did Tatiana's family fly on both airplanes?

   a. 520 miles   b. 633 miles
   c. 705 miles   d. 600 miles

2. Mrs. Chang baked desserts for the school bake sale. She baked 36 brownies, 24 cupcakes, and 48 cookies. How many desserts did Mrs. Chang bake?

   a. 108 desserts
   b. 110 desserts
   c. 246 desserts
   d. 87 desserts

3. Which two answer choices in problem 2 are the least reasonable? Explain. _____
_____

WRITE MATH

Courtney sold tickets to the school play. She sold 193 tickets to students and 327 tickets to parents. Courtney says she sold about 500 tickets. Is Courtney's statement reasonable? Explain.
_____
_____
_____

EXPLAIN IT

---

4. Niko rounded both addends to the greatest place value to estimate the following sum.

   $$\begin{array}{r} 623 \rightarrow 600 \\ + \Box \rightarrow + 200 \\ \hline 800 \end{array}$$

   ALGEBRAIC THINKING
   □×5

   What is the least possible value and the greatest possible value of the missing addend?
   _____

Lesson 11 • Reasonableness and Estimation

Module 2

End of Module Review

Name _____ Class _____ Date _____

Find each sum. Use the Commutative or Associative Property of Addition to write another addition fact. [Lesson 1]

1. 3 + 6

2. (4 + 2) + 6

Find each sum. [Lessons 2, 3, 5, and 7]

3. 5
    7
    + 3
    ___

4. 9 + 1 + 9

5. 17 + 41

6. 52
    + 27
    ____

7. 22 + 53 + 14

8. 30
    16
    + 12
    ____

9. 432
    + 217
    _____

10. 103 + 671

Level D Module 2 • End of Module Review 53

Module 2

Find each sum. Regroup as needed. [Lessons 4, 6, 8, and 9]

11. $\begin{array}{r} 27 \\ +\ 38 \\ \hline \end{array}$

12. $39 + 43$

13. $21 + 64 + 37$

14. $\begin{array}{r} 13 \\ 53 \\ +\ 25 \\ \hline \end{array}$

15. $\begin{array}{r} 345 \\ +\ 278 \\ \hline \end{array}$

16. $782 + 138$

17. $123 + 89$

18. $\begin{array}{r} 479 \\ 42 \\ +\ 35 \\ \hline \end{array}$

Estimate each sum. [Lesson 10]

19. $\begin{array}{r} 279 \\ 510 \\ +\ 67 \\ \hline \end{array}$

20. $\begin{array}{r} 321 \\ 159 \\ +\ 284 \\ \hline \end{array}$

Eliminate unreasonable answers. Solve the problem. [Lesson 11]

21. Fred spent $26 on CDs, $16 on books, and $11 on pens. How much total money did he spend?

    a. $60   **b.** $600

    c. $53   **d.** $10

Extra Practice

Name _____ Class _____ Date _____

Lesson 1 Properties of Addition

Find each sum. Use the Commutative Property of Addition to write another addition fact.

1. 8 + 0
2. 4 + 8
3. 3 + 7
4. 1 + 13
5. 9 + 3
6. 8 + 6

Find each sum. Use the Associative Property of Addition to write another addition fact.

7. (6 + 4) + 1
8. 2 + (4 + 5)
9. 2 + (8 + 8)
10. (5 + 4) + 3
11. 4 + (5 + 6)
12. (1 + 9) + 2

Lesson 2 Adding Three 1-Digit Numbers

Find each sum.

1. 2
   4
   + 1

2. 7
   3
   + 5

3. 3
   6
   + 1

4. 7
   2
   + 7

5. 2
   3
   + 4

6. 2
   8
   + 3

7. 2 + 5 + 2
8. 6 + 1 + 4
9. 9 + 3 + 3
10. 8 + 7 + 1
11. 2 + 3 + 7
12. 1 + 4 + 5
13. 2 + 1 + 8
14. 5 + 8 + 5
15. 12 + 4 + 1

Extra Practice

Name _____ Class _____ Date _____

Lesson 3 Adding 2-Digit Numbers with No Regrouping
Find each sum.

1) 45
  + 12

2) 34
  + 52

3) 19
  + 30

4) 17
  + 32

5) 66
  + 31

6) 21
  + 60

7) 20 + 19

8) 33 + 46

9) 25 + 54

Lesson 4 Adding 2-Digit Numbers with Regrouping
Find each sum. Regroup as needed.

1) 38
  + 14

2) 45
  + 36

3) 28
  + 47

4) 36
  + 24

5) 59
  + 17

6) 45
  + 29

7) 77 + 15

8) 25 + 46

9) 46 + 57

10) 72 + 19

11) 48 + 29

12) 36 + 47

Level D Module 2 • Extra Practice

Extra Practice

Name _____ Class _____ Date _____

Lesson 5 Adding Three 2-Digit Numbers with No Regrouping
Find each sum.

1. 41
    26
  + 11
  ─────

2. 11
    12
  + 13
  ─────

3. 20
    16
  + 31
  ─────

4. 15
    40
  + 22
  ─────

5. 16
    21
  + 50
  ─────

6. 23
    60
  + 15
  ─────

7. 17 + 21 + 30

8. 25 + 13 + 21

9. 40 + 31 + 18

Lesson 6 Adding Three 2-Digit Numbers with Regrouping
Find each sum. Regroup as needed.

1. 23
    19
  + 21
  ─────

2. 54
    77
  + 25
  ─────

3. 39
    16
  + 22
  ─────

4. 32
    45
  + 18
  ─────

5. 61
    18
  + 13
  ─────

6. 45
    17
  + 22
  ─────

7. 54 + 12 + 38

8. 56 + 47 + 25

9. 15 + 32 + 28

Level D Module 2 • Extra Practice   57

Extra Practice

Name _____ Class _____ Date _____

Lesson 7 Adding 3-Digit Numbers with No Regrouping
Find each sum.

1) 121
  + 345

2) 164
  + 211

3) 427
  + 350

4) 675 + 204

5) 562 + 216

6) 165 + 304

7) 274 + 602

8) 500 + 236

9) 164 + 522

Lesson 8 Adding 3-Digit Numbers with Regrouping
Find each sum. Regroup as needed.

1) 439
  + 284

2) 252
  + 369

3) 364
  + 387

4) 518 + 263

5) 384 + 228

6) 655 + 184

7) 236 + 188

8) 756 + 191

9) 346 + 362

Extra Practice

Name _____ Class _____ Date _____

Lesson 9 Adding Multi-Digit Numbers with Regrouping
Find each sum. Regroup as needed.

1.
```
  438
  103
+  54
-----
```

2.
```
  112
   43
+  87
-----
```

3.
```
  210
  186
+  31
-----
```

4.
```
  704
   26
+  65
-----
```

5.
```
  520
+  96
-----
```

6.
```
  643
+  73
-----
```

7. $325 + 934 + 427$

8. $104 + 19$

9. $318 + 25 + 87$

10. $211 + 439 + 164$

11. $60 + 13 + 857$

12. $521 + 74 + 261$

Lesson 10 Estimating Sums
Estimate each sum.

1.
```
  439
+ 284
-----
```

2.
```
  594
+ 312
-----
```

3.
```
   23
+  67
-----
```

4.
```
  454
+ 167
-----
```

5.
```
   55
+  78
-----
```

6.
```
  634
+ 318
-----
```

7. $450 + 165$

8. $655 + 185$

9. $628 + 87$

Extra Practice

Name _____ Class _____ Date _____

Lesson 11 Reasonableness and Estimation

Eliminate unreasonable answers. Solve each problem.

1. Monica's plant was 38 inches tall last year. This year, it grew 18 inches. How tall is Monica's plant now?

  a. 18 inches b. 38 inches

  c. 56 inches d. 86 inches

2. There are 67 students in third grade. There are 55 students in fourth grade. How many students are there in all?

  a. 12 students b. 55 students

  c. 132 students d. 122 students

3. Kevin has 21 crayons, 15 pencils, and 18 pens. How many items in all does Kevin have?

  a. 54 items b. 39 items

  c. 36 items d. 21 items

Glossary

Associative Property of Addition
states that the grouping of the addends can be changed without affecting the sum

Commutative Property of Addition
states that the order of the addends can be changed without affecting the sum

estimate
to find about how many or how much

make a 10
add numbers that make a 10

regroup
to exchange amounts of equal value to rename a number

Name _____ Class _____ Date _____

PROGRESS CHART

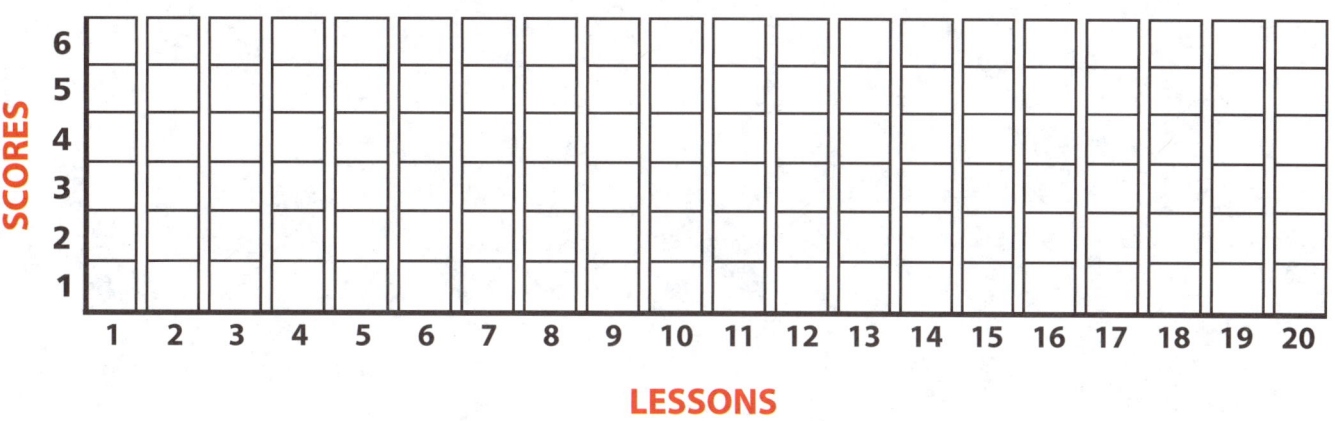